MIXING AND SEPARATING MATERIALS IN MY MAKERSPACE

by Rebecca Sjonger

CRABTREE
PUBLISHING COMPANY
WWW.CRABTREEBOOKS.COM

MATTER AND MATERIALS IN MY MAKERSPACE

Author:
Rebecca Sjonger

Series research and development:
Reagan Miller
Janine Deschenes

Editorial director:
Kathy Middleton

Editor:
Janine Deschenes

Proofreader:
Kelly Spence

Design, photo research, and prepress:
Katherine Berti

Print and production coordinator:
Katherine Berti

Photographs:
iStockphoto: p. 12–13, 27
All other images by Shutterstock

Library and Archives Canada Cataloguing in Publication

Sjonger, Rebecca, author
Mixing and separating materials in my makerspace / Rebecca Sjonger.

(Matter and materials in my makerspace)
Includes index.
Issued in print and electronic formats.
ISBN 978-0-7787-4619-5 (hardcover).
ISBN 978-0-7787-4625-6 (softcover).
ISBN 978-1-4271-2049-6 (HTML)

1. Matter--Properties--Juvenile literature. 2. Materials--Juvenile literature. 3. Makerspaces--Juvenile literature. I. Title.

QC173.36.S57 2018 j530.4 C2017-907636-1
C2017-907637-X

Library of Congress Cataloging-in-Publication Data

Names: Sjonger, Rebecca, author.
Title: Mixing and separating materials in my makerspace / Rebecca Sjonger.
Description: New York, New York : Crabtree Publishing Company, [2018] | Series: Matter and materials in my makerspace | Includes index.
Identifiers: LCCN 2017057957 (print) | LCCN 2018005227 (ebook) | ISBN 9781427120496 (Electronic) | ISBN 9780778746195 (hardcover : alk. paper) | ISBN 9780778746256 (pbk. : alk. paper)
Subjects: LCSH: Matter--Properties--Juvenile literature. | Materials--Experiments--Juvenile literature. | Makerspaces--Juvenile literature.
Classification: LCC QC173.36 (ebook) | LCC QC173.36 .S565 2018 (print) | DDC 530.4--dc23
LC record available at https://lccn.loc.gov/2017057957

Crabtree Publishing Company

www.crabtreebooks.com 1-800-387-7650

Printed in the U.S.A./032018/BG20180202

Published in Canada
Crabtree Publishing
616 Welland Ave.
St. Catharines, Ontario
L2M 5V6

Published in the United States
Crabtree Publishing
PMB 59051
350 Fifth Avenue, 59th Floor
New York, New York 10118

Published in the United Kingdom
Crabtree Publishing
Maritime House
Basin Road North, Hove
BN41 1WR

Published in Australia
Crabtree Publishing
3 Charles Street
Coburg North
VIC 3058

CONTENTS

YOU CAN BE A MAKER!

Makers discover new ways to do tasks. They explore materials. **They experiment and learn as they go. You can be a maker! Keep reading to get started with your own projects that mix, or put together, and separate, or take apart, materials.**

TEAM PLAYERS

Makers often work together so that they can share their ideas, skills, and supplies with each other. **Makerspaces** are places where makers work together. Your school or library may have one. If not, set up your own makerspace with some friends. Get creative together!

No right or wrong!

Makers know:

- The only limit is your imagination.
- Every idea is valuable.
- Things do not always go as planned. Challenges help us learn to solve problems.

Makerspaces have many different materials for you to create with!

MATTER AND MATERIALS

You will mix and separate many materials as a maker. They are all made of matter**. Matter takes up space and has** mass**. Mass is the amount of material in matter. We can find these materials in nature or make them ourselves.**

SOLIDS AND LIQUIDS

This book covers two of the main **states**, or forms, of matter. **Solids** keep their shape. They cannot be poured. This fishbowl is an example of a solid. The water inside it is a **liquid**. Liquids can be poured. They flow into the shape of whatever holds them.

These goldfish are solids, too!

DESCRIBING MATERIALS

Their state is just one of many ways to describe materials. Other characteristics include size or shape. These are known as **properties**. They help makers sort and choose materials. Flip the page to explore more common properties.

The magnifying glass has a round shape.

EXPLORING PROPERTIES

Many properties can be sensed. Try exploring materials with your senses. Ask yourself questions to get started:

- **What does it look like?**
- **Could you taste it or smell it?**
- **Does it make a sound?**
- **What does it feel like when you touch it?**

Ask an adult for permission before you taste or smell any materials, because some can be dangerous.

A scale is a tool that measures an object's **weight**.

MEASURING MATERIALS

You cannot sense every property. You need tools to find some of them. For example, you could measure some properties using a scale or a ruler.

A ruler can measure length, width, and height.

PROPERTY CHALLENGE

Explore materials and their properties to build your maker skills. Get started with these examples:

Is it a liquid or a solid?	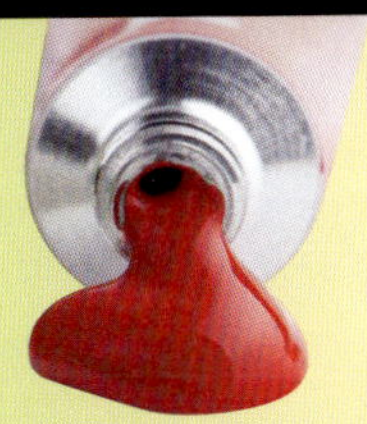		
How hard is it?			
What color is it?			
Does it bend?	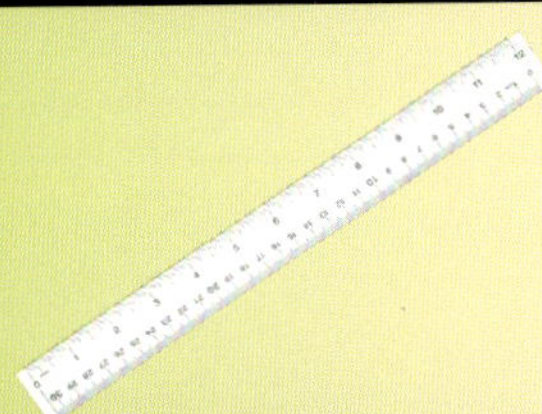		
What does its texture feel like?			
Is it easy to break into pieces?			

You can change the properties of materials. Flip to page 10 to find out how!

MIX IT UP!

Mixing two or more materials makes a mixture. Most matter is a mixture of materials. What happens when you stir cocoa powder into milk? The mixture is chocolate milk. The new, chocolate liquid looks and tastes different from the regular milk and cocoa powder you started with. Its properties changed!

MAKER MATERIALS

Most maker supplies are mixtures. For example, many paints are a mix of liquids. They give a paint its color. They also help it flow and hold its shape. Have you ever mixed two paint colors to make a new one? The mixture had a new color property that could not be undone.

SPLIT THEM UP

You can separate many mixtures. Ask an adult to give you a small amount of salt and pepper. Mix them together with your finger. Use your senses to examine your mixture. Do you sense any changes to the properties of the salt and pepper?

Even when mixed together, the properties of salt and pepper stay the same. The tiny pieces could even be separated! Solids are often easier to separate than liquids.

MAKER TIPS

Are you ready to get started? Kick off each Maker Mission by brainstorming. **Take five minutes to come up with as many ideas as possible. Then, choose one idea to try first. If you work with a team, respect each person's ideas.**

MAKE A PLAN

When you have chosen an idea to try, make a plan that lists the steps you will take to reach your goal. Be open to new ideas along the way! Where you start may not be where your project ends up.

Try making a web to help you organize your ideas. Write your goal in the middle and ideas in the bubbles that branch out.

Makers work together to solve problems and create new things. It is important to respect everyone's ideas.

Help along the way

Mixing and separating materials does not always go smoothly! All makers face challenges. If you get stuck during one of this book's Maker Missions:

- Make sure you understand the goal of the Maker Mission. Try saying the goal in your own words.
- Break up the project into small parts. Work on one part at a time.
- Listen to the ideas of each person on your team. Try to see the mission from a different point of view.

SOLIDS THAT DISSOLVE

What happens to a spoonful of salt when it is mixed with a glass of cold water? Try it! The salt dissolves, or disappears, in the water. It also changes the taste of the water, which becomes salty!

HEAT IT UP

Test what happens when you add heat. Stir a spoonful of salt into a glass of very warm water. Compare how quickly it dissolves to when you used cold water. Higher temperatures often cause solids and liquids to mix faster.

ADD MORE!

Slowly add more and more salt to your glass of water. Use your senses and note how the water changes. See if it is still clear. Does the mixture flow the same way? Try smelling or tasting it!

Try it!

Check out the challenge on the next page to explore other solids that dissolve in water. Try sharing your ideas and supplies with a team.

MAKE A PASTE

MAKER MISSION

Mix a solid and a liquid to make a paste, or a soft, thick substance that can be sticky. Your creation must be sticky enough to hold together two pieces of construction paper. You can also use it in other maker projects!

Materials

- Paper
- Pencil
- Measuring cups
- Mixing bowl
- Whisk or spoon
- Water
- Flour
- Sealable container
- Craft stick
- Construction paper

THINK ABOUT IT

Materials

Which of the solids in the list of materials could you mix into the water?

How would looking at the properties of other pastes or glues help you?

Does the temperature of the water matter?

Size

What amount of solids will you start with? Is it easier to add more solids, or take some away?

Design

How will you spread your paste?

Does the paste need to dry before you test it?

MISSION ACCOMPLISHED

Did your paste join two pieces of construction paper? If it was not sticky enough, what could you change?

When your paste is perfect, check out page 30 for ideas for what to do with it.

SEPARATE WITH SIEVES

Many solids do not dissolve in water. Picture pasta cooking in a pot of water. The hot liquid changes the solid pasta. It becomes soft enough to chew. The materials that make up the pasta do not dissolve, though. The water and pasta do not make a new mixture.

The mixture of materials that make up pasta are called ingredients.

STRAINING LIQUIDS

Cooked pasta must be separated from the water. Have you seen a strainer used in a kitchen? It is a kind of **sieve**. These tools separate liquids and solids. The small holes in sieves are large enough to let liquids through, but not solids.

Liquids and small solids fall through the holes in a sieve. Larger materials stay inside it.

SEPARATING SOLIDS

Another kind of sieve separates solid materials. It is used to sort matter of different sizes. In the past, people used pans with holes in them to separate gold nuggets from sand!

Try it!

You can make your own sieve! Keep reading for your next Maker Mission. Brainstorm as many design ideas as you can to get started.

MAKE IT SORT

MAKER MISSION

Your next challenge is to make a sieve to separate solids and liquids. It must allow liquid to flow through and hold in solid materials.

Materials

- Paper
- Pencil
- Ruler
- Tape
- Hammer and nail
- Plastic container, or a container with a plastic lid
- Solids, such as marbles or rocks
- Scissors
- Pail
- Water

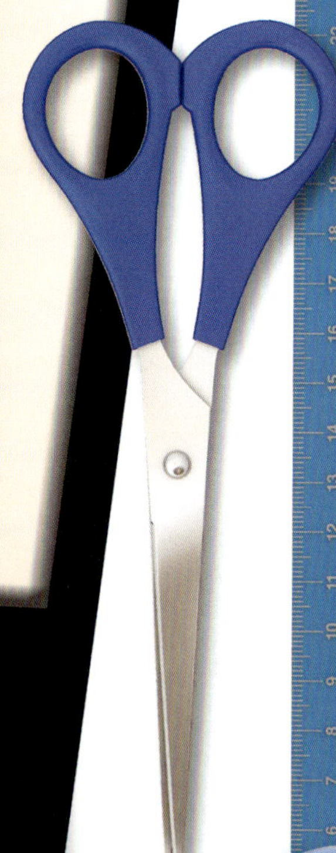

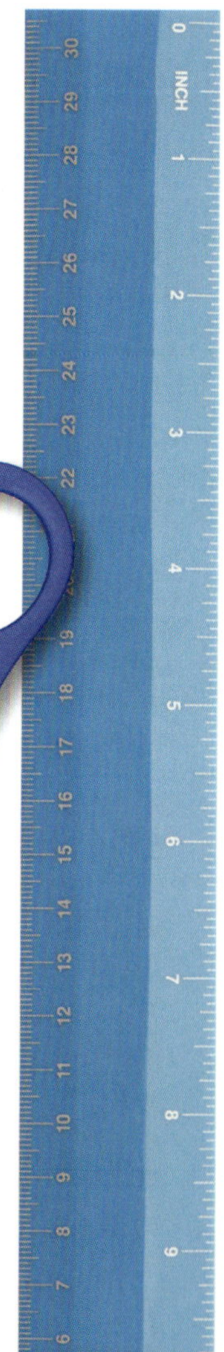

MAKE IT SAFE

Ask an adult for help when making any holes in a container.

THINK ABOUT IT

Materials

Which other recycled materials could be used instead of a plastic container? Will you use a material that already has holes?

Which materials do you need to measure?

What materials could you use to make holes?

Design

Will you make holes in the container's bottom or lid?

How big will your holes be?

How will you test your sieve?

MISSION ACCOMPLISHED

Did your sieve separate solid and liquid materials? If not, look at your design. Go back to the Maker Tips on page 12 if you need help.

When your sieve meets your goals, flip to Endless Ideas on page 30.

DO ALL LIQUIDS MIX?

Remember, some solids dissolve in liquids. Other solids do not change when mixed with liquid. What do you think happens when two or more liquids mix?

NEW MATERIAL

Some liquid mixtures make a new material. Have you ever poured bubble bath into a tub of water? If so, you made a fun material with new properties! The way the water looked, smelled, and even tasted changed. You could not separate the bubbly mixture.

LAYERED MATERIALS

Some liquids do not mix to create a new material. They may look as if they have new properties at first. But something cool happens when the mixture rests for a while. The liquids separate all by themselves!

Lava lamps mix two different types of liquids, but they do not create a new mixture. The liquids float separately in the lamp.

Liquids with different weights often separate into **layers**. Heavier liquids sink. Lighter liquids float on top of them.

Try it!

Watch how liquids separate into layers in the next Maker Mission. Fire up your imagination and go to the next page.

MAKE LIQUID LAYERS

MAKER MISSION

Experiment with liquids to find at least four that do not mix. Your goal is to see the liquids separate into layers.

Materials

- Paper
- Pencil
- Spoons
- Liquids, such as water, vegetable oil, honey, liquid soap, rubbing alcohol, or corn syrup
- Clear test containers, such as glasses or plastic cups
- Glass jar with a screw-on lid

DON'T TICK OFF YOUR PARENTS

Make sure an adult knows which materials you plan to mix. This challenge could get messy! Find a space that is easy to clean up when you are done.

THINK ABOUT IT

Materials

Why should you test which liquids separate before putting them all in your jar?

Do the colors of the liquids matter in this challenge? Why or why not?

Size

Could the size of your container change your results?

Is it important to measure how much of each liquid you use?

Will you use the same amounts of each liquid?

MISSION ACCOMPLISHED

Did you make at least four separated layers? If not, keep mixing! Think about the properties of each liquid you work with.

There are more ideas to try on page 30.

MATERIALS MASH-UP

Flip back through this book. Hunt for ways that change materials when you mix them. Which ones would you like to explore on your own or with a team of friends?

MAKE YOUR OWN MIXTURE

Experiment with mixtures of solids and liquids you find at home or school. Build on what you learned making a paste and layered liquids in the Maker Missions. As you explore and test, look for changes in your materials. For example, note new colors, textures, or smells in mixtures.

BIG BANG!

Sometimes, mixing matter can cause a big reaction. Mixing liquid or solid **chemicals** can lead to explosions! It's important to follow safety instructions when working with any material. Before you mix any materials together, ask an adult for help. To be safe, wear gloves and eye protection.

Always read the labels on materials carefully. Labels can tell us a material's safety risks.

Try it!

Get ready for some fizzy fun! Keep trying new things until you reach your goal in the next Maker Mission.

MAKE IT BUBBLE

MAKER MISSION

Mix vinegar and baking soda to make a new material. Your goal is to create a mixture that bubbles!

Materials

- Paper
- Pencil
- Baking soda
- Vinegar
- Measuring cup and spoons
- Mixing spoon
- Clear container
- Test area container, such as a plastic tub

MAKE IT SAFE

Remember that mixing some materials can be dangerous! Be sure to stick to baking soda and vinegar for this challenge.

THINK ABOUT IT

Materials

Will you use the same amount of both materials?

Size

Does the size of the container matter?

Design

How could testing help you?

Will you test in small or large batches?

Which material will you put in the container first?

Where is the best place to put your test area container?

MISSION ACCOMPLISHED

Did you make a bubbly new mixture? Which other property changes do you see?

Check out more exciting ideas on the next page.

ENDLESS IDEAS

Try mixing and separating your materials in other ways! Which of the ideas below will you make first?

Make a paste

pages 16–17

- Try pasting a mix of paper materials to make a piece of art.
- Experiment with non-paper materials. What else could you stick together with your paste?

Make it sort

pages 20–21

- Which other materials could you experiment with?
- Will you change your test materials or your sieve design?

Make liquid layers

pages 24–25

- What do you think may happen if you drop food dye into your jar?
- Challenge yourself to see how many more layers you can create.
- Add solids, such as glitter or small plastic items. Do they change your mixture?

Make it bubble

pages 28–29

- Now that you have the pretend lava, make a volcano! Use a watery version of the paste you made to try **papier-mâché**.
- Place a container inside your volcano and watch your mixture shoot out!

LEARNING MORE

BOOKS

Claybourne, Anna. *Experiments with Materials*. Windmill Books, 2017.

Oxlade, Chris. *Mixing and Separating*. Crabtree, 2009.

Ross, Michael Elsohn. *What's the Matter in Mr. Whisker's Room?* Candlewick, 2007.

WEBSITES

Learn more about mixing and separating colors at:
www.discoverycube.org/blog/mixing-colors

Try something new and mix materials to make your own play dough:
www.instructables.com/id/How-to-Make-Playdough-Play-doh

To add some fizz to your liquid layers, check out:
www.sciencefun.org/kidszone/experiments/lava-lamp

GLOSSARY

brainstorm To list many ideas—no matter how silly—as quickly as possible

chemical A material made through a scientific process

layer Matter that covers a surface or lies above or beneath another

liquid Matter that can be poured and takes on the shape of its container

makerspace A place where makers work together and share their supplies and skills

mass The measurable amount of material in matter

material Any substance that makes up matter

matter Any material that takes up space and has mass

mixture Two or more materials that are mixed together

papier-mâché A material made with watery glue and paper that can be shaped and hardens when dry

property A characteristic that describes matter

sieve A tool that has holes that separate materials with different properties

solid Matter that does not flow and cannot be poured

state The form that matter takes

texture The look or feel of an object, such as soft or rough

INDEX

ABOUT THE AUTHOR

Rebecca Sjonger is the author of more than 50 children's books. She has written numerous titles for the *Be a Maker*! and the *Simple Machines in My Makerspace* series.